UNIVERSITY OF WOLVERHAMPTON

05/07

Democracy Disrupted

ONE WEEK LOAN

Ivan Krastev

KT-443-503

UNIVERSITY OF PENNSYLVANIA PRESS

PHILADELPHIA

WITHDRAWN

Copyright © 2014 University of Pennsylvania Press

Published by
University of Pennsylvania Press
Philadelphia, Pennsylvania 19104-4112
www.upenn.edu/pennpress

Printed in the United States of America
on acid-free paper

10 9 8 7 6 5 4 3 2 1

Cataloging-in-Publication Record is
available from the Library of Congress

Cover image © Rasslava / 123RF. Cover design by John Hubbard.

ISBN 978-0-8122-2330-9

Contents

Introduction

The European revolutions of 1848 ended on December 2, 1851, when tragedy repeated itself as a farce and Louis Napoleon Bonaparte guillotined the Second French Republic by means of a coup. In the days and weeks during which this last act of the revolutionary drama was unfolding before the eyes of the world, five of the greatest political minds of nineteenth-century Europe ran to their writing desks with the ambition to capture the meaning of the event. They felt they were living in strange times, "when one was never sure, between ordering and eating one's dinner, whether a revolution might not intervene."[1] They wanted to explain to the public what had happened and what could be expected next. The five were very different people with very different political ideas and world views. Karl Marx was a communist. Pierre Joseph Proudhon was an anarchist. Victor Hugo, the most popular French poet and writer of his time, was a romantic. And Alexis de Tocqueville and Walter Bagehot were liberals.[2]

As one would expect from analyses written in the heat of the moment and burdened by passions and frustrations, the authors got the characters of the political actors right but the story wrong. In the manner of the man who mistook his wife for a hat, they mistook the end of the revolutionary wave for its beginning. If the experience of the great five teaches us anything, it is that making sense of the present can be as troublesome as predicting the future.

The desire to make sense of the present is what guided me in writing this little book on protests and democracy. It is not a book about any particular protest, although the protests in Bulgaria inspired me to undertake this adventure, and protests in Russia, Turkey, and Thailand are central to my argument. The book does not attempt to venture an overarching theory of the protests or to conceptualize the new protest experience. It is not a book by somebody who was really *there* or even dreamt of participating in the events it describes. It does not strive to classify the protests or to figure out how to judge their success or failure. Its aim is more modest: to capture the meaning of the events, to reflect on the complex relationship between mass protests and democracy, and to analyze how mass protests are transforming democracy.

In the three short years between Occupy Wall Street and Vladimir Putin's "Occupy Crimea," we witnessed an explosion of protests all around the world—the Arab Spring, Russian Winter, Turkish Summer, and the dismembering of Ukraine all were part of the protest moment. Each of these demonstrations—and many less monumental ones—was angry in its own way, but the protests are also a worldwide phenomenon.

Do they signal a radical change in the way politics will be practiced? Or are they simply a spectacular but ultimately insignificant eruption of public anger? Is it the technology, the economics, the mass psychology, or just the zeitgeist that has caused this global explosion of revolt? Do the protests prove the technologically amplified power of citizens? Or, alternatively, do they mark the decline of the political influence of the middle class and its growing discontent with democracy? Will it be the empowering energy of the protests or the conservative backlash against them that will shape the future of democratic politics?

What strikes any observer of the new wave of revolutionary politics is that it is a revolution without an ideology or a project. Protesting itself seems to be the strategic goal of many of the protests. Failing to offer political alternatives, they are an explosion of moral indignation. In most of the protests, citizens on the street treat politics not so much as a set of issues as a public performance or a way of being in the world. Many protesters are openly anti-institutional and mistrustful toward both the market and the state. They preach participation without representation. The protest movements bypass established political parties, distrust the mainstream media, refuse to recognize any specific leadership, and reject all formal organizations, relying instead on the Internet and local assemblies for collective debate and decision making.

In a way the new protest movements are inspired by mistrust in the elites, empowered by mistrust in leadership, constrained by mistrust of organizations, and defeated by the protesters' inability to trust even each other: "This is an obvious but unspoken cultural difference between modern youth protest movements and those of the past. . . . Anybody who sounds like a career politician, anybody who attempts to use rhetoric, or espouses an ideology, is greeted with visceral distaste."[3]

Mistrusting institutions as a rule, the protesters are plainly uninterested in taking power. The government is simply "them," regardless of who is in charge. The protesters combine a genuine longing for community with a relentless individualism. They describe their own political activism almost in religious terms, stressing how the experience of acting out on the street has inspired a revolution of the soul and a regime change of the mind. Perhaps for the first time since 1848—the last of the pre-Marxist revolutions—the revolt is not against the government but against being governed. It is the spirit of libertarianism that brings together Egypt's antiauthoritarian uprising and Occupy Wall Street's anticapitalist insurrection.

For the protesters, it is no longer important who wins elections or who runs the government, not simply because they do not want to be the government, but also because any time people perceive that their interests are endangered, they plan on returning to the streets. The "silent man" in Taksim Square, Istanbul, who stood without moving or speaking for eight hours, is a symbol of the new age of protests: He stands there to make sure that things will not stay as they are. His message to those in power is that he will never go home.

While it is popular for Europeans to compare the current global protest wave with the revolutions of 1848, today's protests are the negation of the political agenda of 1848. Those revolutions fought for universal suffrage and political representation. They marked the rise of the citizen-voter. The current protests are a revolt against representative democracy. They mark the disillusionment of the citizen-voter. The current protests function as an alternative to elections, testifying that the people are furious;

the angry citizen heads to the streets not with the hope of putting a better government in power but merely to establish the borders that no government should cross.

But is a protest really a better instrument than elections for keeping elites accountable? Can we be confident that people will amass on the streets in large numbers whenever the public interest is violated? Could it not be that the next time the government crosses the line, there will be too few protesters and the effort will fail? How can we be sure that elites will not capture future protests in the same way that they have captured elections? Is the strategy of permanent protest more promising than the once popular dream of permanent revolution?

All these are questions that I have struggled with in this little book. It will be misleading to pretend that I have answered them all, but at least I did not try to neglect them. Some three centuries ago, David Hume was surprised "to see the easiness with which the many are governed by the few."[4] I have been surprised to see the easiness with which the many have risen against the few—and the easiness with which the many have gone home afterward.

Despite their myriad demonstrations of civic courage, creativity, and political idealism, the protests are not the solution to the politics of unconditional demands. They are a form of adjustment to it. In most cases, they have not introduced new political actors or restored trust in politicians or public institutions. On the contrary, the protests have turned a mistrust of institutional norms into a norm of its own. The protests are likewise an insurrection against the institutions of representative democracy but without offering any alternatives within the democratic system or openness to nondemocratic alternatives. The wave of protests is leaderless, finally, not because social media have made leaderless revolutions possible, but because in our libertarian age the ambition to challenge all forms of political representation have made unwelcome political leaders of any stripe. Google's Eric Schmidt thus may well be right when he predicts that "the future will be full of revolutionary movements" but short of "revolutionary outcomes."[5]

Democracy has been disrupted. But to what end? So far, we appear to have no idea—beyond disruption itself.

Protest against Politics

"What is going on?" asked radical French philosopher Alan Badiou two years ago. "Of what are we half-fascinated, half-devastated witnesses? The continuation, at all costs, of a weary world? A salutary crisis of that world . . . ? The end of that world? The advent of a different world?"[1]

The trigger for all these questions has been the massive explosion of protests that has shattered the world since the advent of the Great Recession in 2008. In the last five years, political protests have erupted in more than seventy countries.[2] Some of these, like Egypt and Tunisia, were autocracies; others were democracies like Great Britain and India. Some were prosperous like Israel; others, like Bosnia and Moldova, were poor and depressed. In most of them, social inequality is growing, but in others, like Brazil, it is on the decline. Protests engulfed countries savaged by the global economic crisis—Greece and Portugal being the most notable examples—but they were also found in high-growth emerging economies like Turkey and Russia, which were largely unscathed by the crisis.

To classify is the natural instinct of the social scientist. It is certainly useful to distinguish the prodemocracy protests in places like Tunisia, Egypt, and Russia from the "occupy" movements in the United States, Britain, or Spain. It is useful to distinguish between protests that were organized and directed by opposition parties, like those in Thailand, from protests that were directed against both the government and the opposition, as in Bulgaria and Turkey. It is useful to distinguish between the national revolutions in Ukraine and the antiausterity riots in Greece. All these distinctions are critically important, particularly when we have "big data" about the protests at our fingertips. But we should be also careful not to fall in the trap of too much classifying. It is the protest wave and not any singular protest that provoked Badiou's questions. The cover story of the June 29–July 5, 2013, issue of the *Economist* magazine captured the global nature of the protests. It featured four figures, each representing one of four historical protests and where they took place: 1848, Europe; 1968, America and Europe; 1989, the Soviet Empire; and 2013, "Everywhere."[3]

The protests have been unexpected, spontaneous, and—it must be underscored—nonviolent. Their nonviolence hardly implies an absence of clashes with the police and blood on the streets. We all have witnessed people beaten and killed in Cairo, Istanbul, and Kiev. It means, rather, that the protesters, unlike their revolutionary predecessors, are not attempting a violent takeover. Unlike German or Italian radicals of the 1970s, the protesters of today do not believe in the transformative power of class violence. To bet on violence today for both governments and protesters most often means courting defeat.

It was police violence and brutality that to a great extent explains the mass nature of popular protests in places like Turkey and Ukraine. In the case of Ukraine, the majority of people were unhappy that their government turned its back on the European Union, but it was the decision of this same government to break violently the protest of the pro-European students that brought hundreds of thousands onto the streets. If anything, protesters' strategy of peaceful resistance underscores Erica Chenoveth and Maria J. Srephan's thesis in "Why Civil Resistance Works,"[4] which argues that between 1900 and 2006, nonviolent resistance campaigns were nearly twice as likely to achieve full or partial success as their violent counterparts.

Of course, the reasons for mobilization were contextually distinct. In Tunisia, the self-immolation of the street vendor Mohammed Bouazzi, long harassed by the local police, brought people onto the streets in droves. In Russia, it was the government's manipulation of parliamentary elections coupled with the outrage that the corruption ran to the very top that unleashed the explosion. In Madrid, a combination of rage against rising unemployment and the corruption of the banks and politicians brought young Spaniards to the squares. But the protesters did not land from outer space. Burrowing into the recent history of civic activism reveals layers of small and dispersed protests in which activists and strategists of the current wave were introduced to the art of political rioting. In some countries, the antiglobalization protests helped people find their way to the public squares. In Russia, it was the miniscule marches of the "disbelievers" and the rise of civic activism in 2009. In Bulgaria, it was the environmental protest movements of the last decade that convinced citizens that ultimate gains can be made only when one is ready and willing to challenge authority on the streets. Many who took to the streets of Kiev in the winter of 2014 had been there a decade earlier during the Orange Revolution.

What distinguishes the current protest wave has been its scale. This time, protests have been massive affairs joined by hundreds of thousands of people. Israel was witness to the largest grassroots mobilization in its history. Over two million people participated in the Spanish protests of 2011. More than one million took to the streets in Brazil in 2013. "Sorry for the inconvenience, we are changing the world," was the pumped-up message of the young rebels. Strategy shifted from country to country: some protesters chose to occupy public spaces and claim their own territory; others preferred to deploy the sacred instrument of the daily march to evince their anger. In some countries, the protests were sanctioned by the authorities, in others they were acts of civil disobedience. Although opposition parties and trade unions orchestrated some of the protests, as had been customary in the past, the majority of the most spectacular were led by neither. In many cases, the protests were aimed against these institutions of normal politics and civil society. It was these leaderless protests—in which there were no stages and politicians were silenced— that marked the new wave of unrest.

The demonstrations were different, but the slogans of the protesters were strikingly similar. In all corners of the globe, protesters were appalled by the corruption of the elites, rising social inequality, a lack of solidarity and social justice, and a disrespect for human dignity. Thousands of videos have captured the outrage and disbelief of the Ukrainians who "made a visit" to the abundant private palace of the toppled Ukrainian president Viktor Yanukovych. People were shocked by the mind-blowing combination of luxury and tastelessness that were on display. Elites came out looking like greedy and dishonest liars, cowards, and thieves.

"This is not the crisis, it is the system" has been the battle cry. But while the slogans of the protests were similar, the demands varied. All protesters favored democracy, but in authoritarian states, protesters demanded Western-style democracy and elections, while in the democratic West protesters wanted a different kind of democracy from the one they have. The spread of the protests resembled a flu epidemic. The revolutionary virus of Tunisia was easily caught in Madrid. The white piano that became a symbol of the protests in Istanbul got reproduced in Sofia. In Moscow, Pussy Riot sang: "Egyptian air is good for the lungs / Turn Red Square into Tahrir." The spread of the protests was a demonstration of the primacy of form over content. Bosnians who went on the streets after watching television coverage of the protests in Ukraine were probably poorly informed about what sparked the uprising in Kiev, but they got the underlying message right: political issues today are resolved on the streets. The global spread of the protests was assisted by the visual dimension of politics, since images are more universal and contagious than words.

Ultimately, several protests managed to overthrow governments or blocking certain policies. Others were defeated or ran out of steam. It is instructive that with the passage of time it is increasingly difficult to decide which protests succeeded. Two years after the massive demonstrations in Moscow, Putin remains in the Kremlin and Russia is even less democratic than before. The anti-Putin opposition is demoralized and defeated. In Egypt, the army is back in power and many of those who demanded elections two years ago now praise "the people's coup" of the generals. In the United States, Occupy Wall Street disappeared as dramatically as it emerged. In Greece, resistance against austerity policies has waned. The protest wave in Bulgaria has left the public even more desperate and mistrustful than before. In Ukraine, the country's borders have become uncertain, and the most significant long-term impact of the protests may be the wave of reactionary policies they helped to spawn.

The conventional wisdom of the moment holds that the protests were sparked by social media. Activists planned protests on Facebook, coordinated them via Twitter, spread them by text messages, and webcast them to the world on YouTube. The new social movements conceptualized themselves as networks and became convinced that networks can trump hierarchy. The all-powerful network is their organizational weapon of choice in the same way that the small but disciplined revolutionary party was once the organizational weapon of choice for communists.

But while social scientists have raced to study how social media made the new protest wave possible, there has been surprisingly little interest in how social media also contributed to the rise of protest frustration. A study of Russian social networks after Putin's reelection could give us a frightening picture of the destructive power of social networks and their tendency to turn defeat into catastrophe by provoking cascades of mutual incriminations and waves of conspiracy theories. Governments have been quick to learn how to control and manipulate the masses in a digital world: "Dear subscriber, you are registered as a participant in mass disturbance." This was the message Ukrainian protesters found on their mobile phones in mid-January, 2014, the very moment in which new antiprotest legislation was adopted by the country's parliament. The same technology that brought people to the street was warning them to go home. The government has become every citizen's Facebook friend.

If mass expressions of social fury are indeed a form of a revolution, it is a strange kind of revolution. In the twentieth century, revolutions still had ideological labels. They were "communists" like Vladimir Lenin, "fascists" like Benito Mussolini, or "Islamists" like Ruhollah Khomeini. Law-abiding citizens did not go to sleep before learning which theory had taken to the streets. Today's revolutions are not inspired by theories; they have acquired company names. Pundits speak of "Facebook revolutions," "Twitter insurrections," and "Blackberry riots." Spanish sociologist Manuel Castells called the nameless new protest movements "networks of outrage and hope."[5] They succeeded in capturing the public imagination without engendering a new ideology or charismatic leaders. What these protests will be remembered for are videos, not manifestos; happenings, not speeches; conspiracy theories, not political tracts. They are a form of participation without representation.

The Antipolitics of the Street

"We're in the middle of a revolution caused by the . . . collapse of free market capitalism . . . an upswing in technical innovation, a surge in . . . individual freedom and a change . . . about what freedom means,"[6] avers British journalist Paul Mason, the author of *Why It's Kicking Off Everywhere*, one of the most widely read and inspiring books about the new age of protest. Mason, who acts as a kind of twenty-first-century John Reed of the global anticapitalist class has journeyed to Cairo, Tunisia, and Moscow, and has spent time with the Indignados in Spain, "occupiers" in the United States, and rioters in Athens and London. Out of these travels, he advances two fundamental points: that the anti-Mubarak uprising in Egypt, the occupation of Wall Street, and other manifestations of political unrest are simply different episodes of the same global revolution; and that the revolutionary imagination has returned to politics. If a decade ago "it was easier to imagine the end of the world than the end of capitalism,"[7] today capitalism looks like a dead-end for the majority of young people. Young people today do not see capitalism as their future because they do not see a future for themselves in a world dominated by global capital. They fear that they will have to compete for jobs with machines and that they will be treated like machines. The demographic boom in the global south and the technological boom in the global north inverted the very meaning of "having a job." Most young people do not have a job even when they work. If in the precrisis period a young Spaniard could live with the illusion that his underemployment was his choice—a decision made in freedom to live like an artist—now he knows it is no longer the case. In the next two or three decades, many of the professions to which young people currently aspire will be as unknown as the previously respectable job of stenographer is to us now.

In Mason's view, "the graduate without a future"—the one who has a degree but not a proper job and who has inherited nothing but the debts of the older generation—is the lead protagonist of the new revolution, and the "occupied" public spaces have become workshops for a new generation of democratic politics: a politics without leaders and followers. What matters most for Mason is the revolutionary experience that citizens have gained. In this sense, protests have succeeded in transforming democratic politics even when they have failed to change governments or policies.

Not everyone treats the global protests as a crucible of anticapitalist revolution. We are in the middle of the revolution, agrees American political scientist Francis Fukuyama, but its protagonists are not the losers (graduates without a future) but the winners (citizens empowered by the opening of state borders and the spread of new technologies). Rather than being a crisis of democracy, Fukuyama asserts, the revolution is a triumph of democracy. It is the emergence of a new global middle class defined less by income and more by education, occupation, and lifestyle that has challenged democratic and nondemocratic regimes alike. Fukuyama posits that the recent expansion of the middle class explains the sources and dynamics of the protests. The new revolution is one of expectations not of frustrations. This is why it is not anomalous that the protests have hit hard some of the economically most successful countries and those least affected by the financial crisis of 2008.

Beyond expectations, the emerging global middle class is empowered by new digital technologies and characterized by its mobility and individualism. These individuals live in a world governed by global comparisons. The medical doctor in Brazil is no longer satisfied to compare his lot in life to his neighbor working in the local shop; rather, his point of comparison is with his colleagues in Berlin or Singapore. He insists on his "right" to have better public services and to have far more control over his life. He demands new norms for transparency and accountability, and political elites are pressed to make good on them. This new "civic vigilantism" is simply another expression of the general trend toward the democratization of public life. What makes this middle-class revolution principally different from its nineteenth-century predecessors is that this time the global middle class is far more attached to the market than to the nation-state. Protesters on the streets do not want to overthrow democratic governments, they want to control them.

Fukuyama has a point. But in two important aspects, the current discussion of the middle class is different from the twentieth-century debate about the historical role of the national bourgeoisie. In the last century, the aristocracy was the symbol of a cosmopolitan identity; the middle class, by contrast, was identified with the interest of the nation-state, and state nationalism was its customary political ideology. This is no longer the case. What is different today is an apparent schism within the middle class. There exists a *statist middle class* (a national bourgeoisie), usually represented by government functionaries and low- and middle-level managers of public companies who aspire to be part of the government; and then there is a *global libertarian middle class* whose political ambition is not to be in government, but rather to control it. This global middle class is suspicious of any government. It believes that it has succeeded in life not because of anything the state has provided but against the attempts of the state to put its grubby hands on everything.

Those in the global middle class and those in the statist middle class often share similar income and educational levels, but they see the world very differently. The state-dependent middle class is highly anxious about the shrinking of the state; the global middle class prays for it, and it is the latter that is at the heart of today's protests in many parts of the world. The protesters in Moscow who labeled themselves "the creative class" and the Bulgarian protesters who were dubbed "the smart and the beautiful" are both representatives of the mobile and more cosmopolitan part of the middle class that trusts the market more than the state even when it subscribes to anticapitalist, anticonsumerist slogans.

Paradoxically, the protest is not so much a means of defending the interests or the values of the middle class. It is a way of preserving the status of the middle-class individual at the time when in many parts of the world his income has been painfully hurt by the economic downturn. It was mesmerizing to observe philosophy professors from the University of Sofia marching for months against the government and thus preserving their social and political identity at the very moment when they are paid ridiculously low salaries and when the conventional wisdom holds that philosophers have become obsolete. In their book *Identity Economics*, George Akerlof and Rachel Kranton assert that identity may be the most important "economic" decision a person ever makes. This observation is critical for understanding the nature of the middle-class protests.[8] People do not protest because they *are* middle class but because they want to be—and because they know that in situations like this, middle-class individuals should be on the streets. Political activism compensates for the economic impossibility of being middle class in the midst of an intractable recession.

Do the protests signal a radical change in the way politics will be practiced? Or are they simply a spectacular but ultimately insignificant eruption of public anger? "Is it the technology, the economics, the mass psychology, or just the zeitgeist that's caused this global explosion of revolt?"[9] Do the protests make clear the new power of the citizen or, alternatively, do they mark the decline of the political influence of the middle class and its growing discontent with democracy?

Suzanne Collins's best-selling trilogy *The Hunger Games*—the story of a rebellious girl, Katniss Everdeen, who raises hell and brings a revolution in a land where revolution had been defeated seventy-five years earlier—captures the new spirit of rebellion better than faddish sociological theories. The global protests, like Katniss's revolution, boil down to an insurgency that is antipolitical at its base. It is born out of a profound sense of injustice, governed by a broad array of images, and rooted in an innate sense of empathy and human solidarity. The conscience-stricken celebrity may be its only legitimate leader. Is it accidental that Kseniya Sobchak—the enfant terrible of Moscow's good society, who is famous for little more than being famous—became one of the symbols of Russia's protests? It is a revolution without an ideology or a master plan. It does not envision a future radically different from the world of today. Failing to offer political alternatives, it is an explosion of moral indignation. Protesters are furious that their freedom does not translate into a capacity to change aspects of their socioeconomic condition that they desperately want to change. That leaves rebellion as the only option.

In this sense, the protests of today are in some sense a 3-D remake of the revolution of 1968, though in another sense they are strikingly different. In 1968, revolutionary students around the world experimented with drugs and free love, but they were also committed to understanding how the system worked. The system was their obsession. Reporting on the occupation of Columbia University that year, the poet Stephen Spender was impressed by the "nervous revolutionary seriousness of the rebels." It was a revolution of sociology students arriving straight from secondhand bookstores. The radicals spent sleepless nights reading and discussing Marx, Mao, and Marcuse.

Today, hardly anybody is interested in the system. The current revolution is not a revolution of readers. Radical students today are only preoccupied with how they experience the system—not by what kind of system it is. Barely thinking in terms of social groups, they have a shared experience but no collective identity. In the "Appeal from the Sorbonne" endorsed in Paris in June 1968, the students of the time spoke of themselves as "privileged persons because we alone have the time, the material, and physical chance to understand our state and the state of our society." Students today, by contrast, do not have a sense of privilege. When they protest at the university, they fail to act on behalf of those who are even less qualified to understand the system. The closest the revolutionaries have come in making a sociological argument is when they denounce the blood-sucking elites of the 1 percent. The government, meanwhile, is simply a conspiracy in power that can be opposed but not really understood. The protesters' view of the system is really not much different from Collins's teenage-inspired antiutopia in which modern society is essentially a high-tech version of the Middle Ages as seen from the standpoint of an illiterate peasant.

In most of the protests, citizens on the street treat politics not as a set of issues but as a kind of performance art. The uprising has the absorbing trance-like quality of a communal hallucination. Protesters are openly anti-institutional and mistrustful toward both the market and the state. They oppose social inequalities but they are against income redistribution as well, believing that sharing with others is a personal decision and should not be a government policy. Many of the citizens of the occupied squares will be ready to break bread with their neighbor but would be reluctant to allow the government to raise middle-class taxes. Reflecting on the political logic of the summer protest in São Paulo, Brazilian researcher Pablo Ortellado observed that demonstrators were protesting all over Brazil with two simultaneous and paradoxical messages: "Government does not represent us" and "We want better public services." It was more of a radical consumers protest than a protest of radical utopians.

Protesters are angry individuals. They enjoy being together, they enjoy fighting together, but they do not have a collective project. It is a revolution brought by indignation and led by hope in which everyone feels tempted to participate. Both the Far Left and the Far Right feel equally at home in this revolution; after all, it is a revolution of good people against bad rulers—the authentic revolution of the 99 percent. As the great anarchist Pierre-Joseph Proudhon wrote in the 1840s, "to be governed is to be kept in sight, inspected, spied upon, directed, law-driven, numbered, enrolled, indoctrinated, preached at, estimated, valued, censured, commanded, by creatures who have neither the right, nor the wisdom, nor the virtue to do so."[10] We are living through the world's first libertarian revolution.

The mass protests revolt against the politics of representation, and not simply those representatives who happen to be in office today. People no longer trust that politicians will represent their interests and ideals. The success of the revolution lies in the people's readiness to return to the square any time needed and by any means necessary.

If our protesters are haunted by the question of what comes next, they can do little better than to read the classic texts of the American social scientist Albert O. Hirschman. Hirschman was born in Berlin in 1915—a rotten time and a wrong place to be Jewish and progressive. When he was nineteen years old, persecution, intolerance, and war decimated the cosmopolitan world that many of his generation had fought to defend. Hirschman left Germany, fought in Spain, smuggled people out of occupied France, and ended up in the United States as one of the most distinguished experts on Latin America and the problems of economic development. Unsurprisingly for someone who constantly mediated the nuances between leaving, fighting, and accepting, Hirschman was preoccupied by two fundamental questions: Why do people engage or disengage in public welfare? And how do people bring about social or political change?

Reflecting on the loss of the revolutionary spirit in France just a decade after the cataclysmic uprisings of May 1968, Hirschman began to ask whether our societies are somehow predisposed to oscillation between periods of intense preoccupation with public issues and the near total concentration on individual improvements and private welfare goals—and he suggested that there are indeed collective cycles of engagement: periods in which people will protest for months followed by a collective withdrawal from public action. If Hirschman's intuition is right, even a successful popular protest hardly guarantees that the next time citizens will return to the streets. The natural outcome of any period of revolutionary idealism will be the desire to return to the values of private life. And digital media will not change this.

How people bring about change was the second question that focused Hirschman's mind. In his most famous work, *Exit, Voice, and Loyalty*, he contrasted the two strategies that people have for dealing with poorly performing organizations and institutions. People can either "exit"—that is, voting with their feet by expressing their displeasure by taking their business elsewhere—or decide to "voice" their concerns by staying put, speaking up, and choosing to fight for reform from within. In his reading, exit is the path to reform favored by economists because it is the preferable strategy of the consumer. By inflicting revenue losses on delinquent management, exit is expected to induce a "wonderful concentration of the mind" akin to what Samuel Johnson attributed to the prospect of being hanged. Hirschman knew that in many cases exit works well, but he also pointed out that "those who hold power in the lazy monopoly may actually have an interest in creating some limited opportunities for exit on the part of those whose voice might be uncomfortable." In short, forcing (or simply allowing) his critics to leave the country may be the best strategy for a dictator. Exit can bring reform, but under certain conditions, it can also become a major obstacle for reforming society.[11]

Voice represents a different type of activism, one where people cannot or simply do not want to exit because they deeply value the organization in crisis. Instead, they are compelled to improve its performance by participating, offering ideas, and taking the risk to oppose those who make decisions. Voice-led activism is constructive by its very nature. It assumes a readiness to take responsibility for what one suggests. It is closely associated with the strategy to change an organization, party, or church from within, and it is based on loyalty. For loyalists, to exit means to desert. In this sense, voice is never synonymous with simply *opposing* power; it assumes the responsibility to *be* the power.

As any social scientist will tell you, exit and voice can be complementary under certain conditions. But they can also function as diametric opposites. Could it be that collective political mobilizations like the mass street demonstrations of the past few years—those protests that are celebrated as evidence of civil society's revival and that we presume to be prototypical expressions of voice—are in fact a form of exit that instead of challenging the status quo end up reinforcing it?

A Tale of Two Antiprotests

Bulgaria's demonstrations in 2013 can serve as a telling case study of today's global protest movement, especially in what they reveal about that movement's antipolitical character. Bulgaria is a small and somewhat obscure post-communist country. Rarely does it hit the front pages of international newspapers. Since the fall of communism in 1989, it has become freer, slightly more prosperous, and far more unequal. It has become messier, too—a prime candidate for *protest vote democracy*, with high electoral volatility in which governments are never reelected but economic policies are rarely changed. In the last twenty-five years, Bulgaria has been governed by the Left (ex-communists), by the Right (anticommunists), from above (when former King Simeon Saxe-Coburg-Gotha won the 2001 elections and became prime minister) and from below (when the former head of the same king's security detail, the erstwhile firefighter, Boyko Borrissov, left the king's party, founded his own, and won the 2009 elections). Thus Bulgaria has experienced a permanent rotation of those in power, but if you listen to the man and woman on the street, the people in power have remained the same.

In 2013, the country was wracked by protests. In February, hundreds of thousands of Bulgarians, mostly low-income folk from the countryside, stormed the streets to protest a hike in electricity prices and a deteriorating standard of living. The protests began in the provincial city of Blagoevgrad, where some one thousand people, mobilized through social media, gathered after work in front of the offices of the foreign-owned electricity company, waving their bills (together with their national flags). Over the course of a week, the "uprising of the electricity bills" went viral and spread to thirty-five cities and municipalities. Day after day citizens took to the streets and public squares, accusing the electricity companies of ripping them off, declaring their inability to pay their bills, and blaming the government for doing nothing to improve the situation.

The high electricity bills became the symbol of everything that was wrong with the postcommunist order: privatization leading to inside deals for the well connected, a corrupt and inefficient state bureaucracy, and a political elite unconcerned with the struggles of the people. Proposals for how to respond to the crisis, at least from the street, were contradictory, ranging from nationalization of the utilities to more market competition. Still, the message was clear: people did not believe that their interests were represented by the government. Opposition politicians and trade union leaders were deliberately sidelined from the protests. Television became a mark of inauthenticity, as people refused to trust anyone they had seen on it. However, experts were not the only casualty; cultural celebrities were also excluded from the protests. While the major television channels covered them extensively, it was clear that protesters were unrepresented not only by the political parties but also by Western-funded NGOs brimming with experts who brazenly volunteered to speak on their behalf. People on the streets were "nobody voters," not because they had not voted in previous elections but because they had voted practically for everyone they were now seeking to depose. The politicians had forfeited their right to rule by failing accurately to represent the voters. It was a revolt of "desperate men . . . altogether abandoned, not only by Fortune, but even by Hope."[12]

Following the violent clashes between the protesters and the police, the center-right government of Borrissov resigned. But the protesters were in no hurry to celebrate the resignation of the government as a victory. Early elections were glaringly absent from their priority list. What they wanted was not early elections but higher pay and greater purchasing power. They had learned over the years that it was easier to get something from the government just before elections than after them. But this time they got elections without any improvement in the standard of living.

In many respects, the February protests are a reminder of riots during the Middle Ages, when people went to the streets not with the aim of overthrowing the king but rather to force the king to change his policies and make life bearable. Having learned that in Bulgaria a change of government changes nothing at all, the people acted out in a desperate attempt to get noticed and provoke some kind of reaction or break from the status quo.

Then suddenly, on June 14, just two weeks after the election of a new center-left government, tens of thousands of citizens, mostly representatives of Sofia's middle class, took to the streets again.[13] This time it was the educated citizens who were provoked into action by the decision of the new government to appoint Delyan Peevski, a young media mogul with shady contacts and an even worse reputation, as the head of the national security agency, the governmental body entrusted to fight organized crime and corruption. The appointment of Peevski was perceived as a direct and blatant offense to the national body politic. Not only was it bad politics, but it also showed bad taste. The newly appointed anticorruption czar looked straight out of central casting as the bad guy in a low-budget American movie. At the tender age of twenty-one, he had been appointed a member of the board of a major company. In his late twenties, he became deputy minister and later a member of parliament. He drove expensive cars, traveled in the company of a small army of personal bodyguards, and only rarely set foot in the parliament or participated in any public discussions and was believed to have power over at least part of the judicial system. His own mother controlled most of the country's newspapers. He soon became the hated symbol of the nasty intersection between shady business practices and politics, the sinister "them" who actually governs the country—a ruler you cannot change through elections.

A certain invisible line dividing the tolerable from the intolerable had been crossed with this egregious appointment. For the urban middle class, the government's choice was symbolic of everything that is wrong with the country's political system. The shadowy power of business interests hearkened back to the old communist power structures and demonstrated the lack of competition and disrespect for democracy among members of the political elite. People stormed the streets demanding the resignation of the government and early elections. What they got was the resignation of the young hoodlum and a reduction of electricity prices.

Bulgaria's February and June protests were in many ways replicas of each other. Both were spontaneous eruptions of public anger directed against the political elite, organized by neither opposition parties nor trade unions.

Both refused any form of political representation that would allow someone to speak on behalf of the protesters. Both were generally peaceful and directed against the degradation of democratic politics. Both included declarations of a turning point in Bulgarian politics and demands for a new constitution and electoral laws. Both saw a majority of the public supportive of the protester's demands.

But the two protests were also very different. In his insightful article, "Bulgaria's Year of Civic Anger," political scientist Venelin Ganev distinguishes between two kinds of circumstances that mobilize people to enter the public arena. One is a form of poor governance understood as policy failure (e.g., one that results in unbearable electricity prices), the other is a threat to the democratic nature of the political system when people lose the conviction that they live in a democracy[14]. In his study of protests in eighteenth- and nineteenth-century China, Ho-fung Hung makes a complementary point, distinguishing between "state-engaging" and "state-resisting" protests. State-engaging protests look to the state for redress or protection; state-resisting protests defend existing resources and activities from state interference.[15] In this sense, the two Bulgarian protests of 2013 had different etiologies— they arose from distinct sources and had distinct expectations from the state.

The June protests fit the notion of a global middle-class revolution. The February protests, which were more radical, did not. The winter protesters were hostile to foreign investors and not a single European flag was flown at their demonstrations. The headquarters of foreign companies were attacked. The people demanded that private monopolies be broken up. The mobilization was highly nationalistic, but it was not the nationalism of thugs but the nationalism of betrayed majorities. The protesters used national sentiments as a way to influence elites and make them accountable. They openly accused the government of governing like foreigners and in the interest of foreigners. What they hoped for was the return of the state as a defender of the national community.

The summer protests spoke a very different language. They referred to a transnational idea of political community in order to secure the accountability of the elites. They were arty; they flew European flags almost everywhere. The June protesters were not asking the government to take care of them not because they were Bulgarians but because they were Europeans. It was belonging to the EU that justified their claims.

Unlike the February protests, however, the people on the streets were not so much nonvoters or people who changed their vote at every election, but politically active citizens who felt unrepresented. It was a protest that early on tried to portray itself as a revolt of an urban middle class squeezed between the arrogance of the oligarchs and the misery of the majority. In an effort to distinguish itself from the February protest, the June protests were dubbed "the protest of the smart and the beautiful." Marches took place after the end of the working day because most of the protesters had jobs. What you could often see during the June protests were young parents with small children. People were railing against corruption and the emerging oligarchic rule but the real crisis was a crisis of the future. The urban middle class did not demand the government to do something for them. Their demand was to control the government.

There was something exciting and purifying about the protests. They were also dispiriting. The majority of the public supported the protesters, but the protesters themselves felt no urge to open their ranks to those from outside the middle classes who thought of themselves as victims. What they lacked though was empathy. They blamed the February protesters for voting all those years for the wrong parties and the wrong leaders. They were convinced that demands for more dramatic social reforms would only pollute their efforts. What they longed for, in some neoromantic way, was for the nation to be transformed into a moral community. It was easier for them to talk to other Europeans, like the French and German ambassadors in the country, than to those of their fellow citizens who did not share their civic anger.

What was most striking in both February and June was the wholesale separation of electoral politics and protest antipolitics. The February protests succeeded in toppling the center-right government and in bringing on early elections, but it was the governing party that captured most of the votes. The election results were exactly those predicted by the pollsters before the protests. If somebody was simply following the dynamics of polling data without paying attention to headlines in the papers, she would never have guessed that major protests had taken place between February and the May elections and that more than 75 percent of the public supported them.

The story of the June protests is quite similar. While almost 70 percent of the population demanded early elections, pollsters predicted once again that the governing coalition would be reelected. Not a single major new party of any import emerged from either the February or the

June protests. How is it possible that in a country where voters had always succeeded in changing the government, the explosion of civic anger did not affect the electoral choices of the citizens? What went wrong with the elections?

The Bulgarian puzzle suggests several interesting hypotheses to be explored. First, in democratic countries, the people are revolting not only against the elites but also against the electoral democracy that has become the system for perpetuating the power of those elites. Second, it suggests that in a situation of growing mistrust toward political elites, people view popular mass protests not as a way to correct electoral democracy but as an alternative to it. Finally, there may actually be an inverse relationship between mass protests and the emergence of new radical parties that aim at fundamental concrete change of the political system. Is it accidental that in countries that have seen massive protests, like Spain and Bulgaria, no radical party has emerged, while in Italy, where no protest took place, a popular radical protest party (Grillo's Five Star Movement) has been formed? It is almost as if the dramatic actions on the streets are more a substitute for politics than an expression of politics.

We are witnessing a cry of frustration against political representation that has no interest in attempting an alternative to the existing forms of representation—that is, beyond the cry of frustration itself. The protests position themselves as an alternative to electoral democracy because the protesters have lost faith in electoral democracy. But what is the alternative? The protesters themselves have no suggestions, beyond acting out. But is democracy organized around never-ending social mobilization going

31

to be more satisfying than those organized around regular elections? Will the next wave of protest be less peaceful? Why are protesters uninterested in elections and why are leaderless protests unable or unwilling to form political parties? How have most government managed to survive amid explosions of public anger? Should unpopular governments fear protests? Or should they view them, surprisingly, as their best means to stay in power?

What seems clear are a series of aporias. The protesting citizen wants change, but he rejects any form of political representation. He longs for political community, but he refuses to be led by others. He is ready to take the risk of being beaten or even killed by the police, but he is afraid to take the risk of trusting any party or politician. He is dreaming of democracy, but he has lost faith in elections.

Chapter 2

The Democracy of Rejection

In *The Watcher*, one of Italo Calvino's early novels, the great writer spins a tale of an election suffused with madness, passion, and reason. The protagonist, Amerigo Ormea, an unmarried leftist intellectual, agrees to be an election monitor in Turin's famous Cottolengo Hospital for Incurables—a home for the mentally ill and disabled. Taking on the role is Ormea's circuitous way to join the struggle. Ever since voting became obligatory in Italy following World War II, places like Cottolengo had served as a great reservoir for right-wing Christian Democratic votes. The hospital thus serves as a vivid illustration of the absurd nature of bourgeois democracy.

During the election, newspapers are filled with stories about invalids being led to vote; voters eating their ballots; and the elderly, paralyzed by arteriosclerosis, pressured to vote for conservative candidates. It is in Cottolengo Hospital that leftist critics of democracy can show that in bourgeois society elections are less about people governing than about elites manipulating them. The image of mentally ill people voting has been used by critics of democracy at least since Plato to demonstrate the farcical nature of democratic governance, a system in which the "sane" and "insane" enjoy equal powers.

Ormea is in Cottolengo to do what he can to prevent the sick, the disabled, and the dead from influencing the election's outcome. His responsibility as an election monitor is to keep pious nuns voting from in place of their patients. It looks like a simple job, but with the passage of time Ormea starts to doubt whether it is the proper thing to do. It is in this very place that the young leftist intellectual, attracted by Marxism and sympathizing with communists, falls under democracy's spell. He is mesmerized by the ritual of elections, of ceremonial pieces of paper folded over like telegrams triumphing over fascists. Ormea is fascinated with the ability of elections to give meaning to human life and make everyone equal, and with how a Christian Democratic senator puts his fate in the hands of Cottolengo's nurses much like a dying man places his fate in the hands of God.

What he finds most striking is the unimaginable egalitarianism of democracy—the fact that rich and poor, educated and illiterate, those ready to die for their ideas and those who have no ideas, all of them have just one ballot and their vote has equal power. Elections resemble death because they force you to look both backward and forward, to judge the life you have lived so far and to imagine another. That is one reason Ormea is struck by the transformational power of democracy. Both Christian Democrats who believe in a divine order and Communists who believe in the dictatorship of the proletariat should have little faith in democracy, but they are its most zealous guardians. It is in the hospital for the incurables that Ormea detects democracy's genius to turn madness into reason and to translate passions into interests.

It is not in democracy's capacity to represent citizens but its talent at misrepresenting them that makes Ormea a believer. The vote gives every citizen equal voice, which means that the intensity of a voter's political opinions are irrelevant. The vote of the fanatic for whom elections are an issue of life and death has the same power as the vote of a citizen who barely knows for whom to vote or why. The result is that voting has a *dual character*—it allows us to replace those in power, thus protecting us from the *excessively repressive state*, but it also takes no measure of popular passions, thereby defending us from the *excessively expressive citizen*. Democracy allows mad people to vote and it could even elect them (though it surely would not tolerate them for long), but it also disarms their madness.

Democracy at once restrains the intensity of political actors while overdramatizing the stakes of the political game. It tries to inspire the apathetic to interest in public life while simultaneously cooling down the passion of the zealot. Mobilizing the passive and pacifying the outraged—these are two of the primary functions of democratic elections. But elections also have a transcendental character. They ask us to judge politicians not simply on what they have done but on what they promise to do. In this sense, elections are a machine for the production of collective dreams. Ban elections and you consent to live in a present without a future—or you subscribe to a future decreed by the state. Elections give us a hand in constructing the future. They bring change; they do not foreclose. They also play a critical role in resolving generational differences by siding, ever so slightly with the young. First-time voters invariably capture the imagination of the politicians, who hope and presume that these new political participants will tilt the balance of power in some new, decisive way, helping to resolve the society's most intractable problems or crises one way or another.

Alexis de Tocqueville was one of the first to suggest that the discourse of crisis is the native language of any genuine democracy. Democratic politics, he observed, need drama: "As the election approaches," Tocqueville wrote, "intrigue becomes more active and agitation lively and more widespread. The entire nation falls into a feverish state . . . As soon as fortune has pronounced . . . everything becomes calm, and the river, one moment overflowed, returns peacefully to its bed."[1]

David Runciman recently suggested that "Tocqueville discovered on his American journey [that] democratic life is a succession of crises that turn out to be nothing of the sort."[2] Democracy thus operates by framing the normal as catastrophic, while promising that all crises are surmountable. Democratic politics functions as a nationwide therapy session where voters are confronted with their worst nightmares—a new war, demographic collapse, economic crisis, environmental horror—but are convinced they have the power to avert the devastation. Politicians and the media will portray almost any election as a turning point—as a choice that will define the fate of the nation for the next generation. Yet when the election is over, the world magically returns to normal.

Democratic politics is impossible without a persistent oscillation between excessive overdramatization and trivialization of the problems we face. Elections lose their cogency when they fail to convince us both that we are confronting an unprecedented crisis and that we have it in our power to avert it.

As political scientist Stephen Holmes has observed, for elections to work, the stakes should be neither too high nor too low. Recent developments in Iraq and Afghanistan are a classical demonstration that when the stakes are too high citizens opt for guns instead of ballots. On the other hand, when nothing important will be decided on Election Day, when elections lose their drama, citizens cannot be bothered to participate. Some of Europe's democracies currently suffer from a crisis of democracy caused by low stakes. Why should the Greeks or Portuguese go to vote when they know perfectly well that the policies of the next government will be identical to the current one? In the days of the Cold War, citizens would go to the ballot box with the expectation that their vote would decide their country's fate: whether it would remain part of the West or join the East, whether industry would be nationalized, and so on. Large, imposing questions were the order of the day. Today, the differences between left and right have essentially vanished and voting has become more a matter of taste than of ideological conviction.

Almost sixty years after the fictional Amerigo Ormea fell under the spell of democracy in Cottolengo Hospital, elections are not only losing their capacity to capture the imagination of the people but also failing to effectively overcome crisis. People have begun to lose interest in them. There is a widespread suspicion that elections have become a "trap for fools." It is true that they have gone global (freer and fairer than ever before), and that we vote more often than in the past, but elections are no

37

longer mobilizing the passive and pacifying the outraged. The decline of electoral turnout throughout all Western democracies over the last thirty years, and the eruption of mass political protests in the last five years, is the most powerful manifestation of the crisis. Elections, in short, have become an afterthought in most of Europe. Just as bad, they give birth to governments mistrusted from their very first day in office. The latest Euro-barometer opinion polls testify that more than 70 percent of Europeans do not trust their national governments—a major change compared with a decade ago.

Political scientists in the United States contend that in a world of growing social inequality, the idea of "one man, one vote" is becoming farce, since the rich people have the financial means to influence the political system far more than the average voters. There are a growing number of people who believe that modern democracies are evolving into oligarchical regimes covered over by a facade of democratic institutions. It is thus no surprise that those most reluctant to take part in elections are the young, poor, and unemployed—those who, in theory, should be most interested in redressing the injustices of the market with the power of the ballot. There is a growing feeling that only money is represented in legislatures.

But the problem with elections is not simply that they leave the underprivileged underrepresented. Thanks to the fragmentation of the public sphere, elections are also failing to produce governing majorities and policy mandates. In 2012, among the thirty-four members of the Organization for Economic Co-operation and Development (i.e., the club of wealthy nations), only four featured a government supported by an absolute majority in the parliament. If elections do not come with clear majorities and unambiguous policy mandates, this accelerates the voters' belief that they are no longer obliged to support the government for which they have voted. This is exacerbated by the reality that even when in the government, parties have a hard time making good on their promises.

The paradoxical effect of the loss of drama in elections is their mutation into a ritual of humiliation to the party in power rather than a vote of confidence in the opposition. These days it would be miraculous to find a government that enjoys the support of the majority only a year after being elected. The dramatic decline of support to French president François Hollande, whose support has dropped by 30 percentage points while nothing extraordinary has happened in France, is a perfect demonstration that if the link between the government and its supporters once resembled an unhappy but solid Catholic marriage, now a government's relationship with voters more resembles a one-night stand. Voters simply do not see their ballot as a long-term contract with the party they have chosen. No longer predicated on one's future expectations, voting is now purely a judgment on past performance.

Unsurprisingly, studies in Europe show that the advantages enjoyed by incumbents are disappearing. Governments are collapsing more quickly than before, and they are reelected less often.[3] "No one is truly elected anymore," Pierre Rosanvallon has argued. "Those in power no longer enjoy the confidence of the voters; they merely reap the benefits of distrust of their opponents and predecessors"[4] In several of the new democracies in Europe, it is easier to "resurrect" than to reelect.

There is another perverse effect of this diminution of drama: elections are failing to demobilize the opposition. Traditionally, electoral victory meant that the winning party would be allowed to govern. Like war, elections had clear winners and losers where the winners imposed their agenda, at least for a while. The opposition could fantasize about revenge, but it was ill-advised to prevent the government from governing. But this is now changing. When parties fail to win majorities or lose them a day after taking office, it is natural that opposition parties will feel emboldened. The proliferation of elections—parliamentary, local, regional, presidential, the pervasiveness of public opinion polls, and the new appetite for referenda make it easy for the opposition to claim that the government has lost—or never won—a popular mandate.[5]

American politics in the age of the populist Tea Party may be the most colorful demonstration of logic of the new order. The Tea Party acts like a guerrilla movement out to savagely impair members of victorious parties—whether Democrats or less doctrinaire Republicans—and keep them from governing effectively. Then that poor performance serves as evidence for the Tea Party's anti-government agenda the next time around. Instead of furthering democracy, elections become occasions for subverting democratic institutions, including elections. The act of voting for candidates is losing its luster for many reasons, but not the least of them is that electoral victory is not what it used to be.

Elections and Futility

The paradox of the current protest wave is that it is a revolt of nonvoters. It is the revolt of those who abstained from voting during the last elections or, perhaps worse, do not even remember for whom they pulled the lever. It is also a revolt of those who believe that voting makes no difference; citizens stay away from the voting booth in order not to encourage *them* (the elites). "I have never voted," confesses the comedian Russell Brand, one of the icons of the new revolution. "Like most people, I regard politicians as frauds and liars and the current political system as nothing more than a bureaucratic means for furthering the augmentation and advantages of economic elites. Imagining the overthrow of the current political system is the only way I can be enthused about politics."[6] In Bulgaria, it turned out that the majority of those who supported the June protests, who demanded the resignation of the government and insisted on early elections, went on to declare in polls that they did not plan to vote in the very elections they requested.[7]

If we want to grasp the nature of the protest wave, we should look much closer at the consequences and implications of the decline of elections. Are popular protests a new institution meant to control politicians between elections (a gentler version of violent insurrections)? Or are they an alternative to electoral politics itself?

Historically the rise of the political influence of the middle class has been bound up with the struggle for universal suffrage. Elections were for the middle class what chess was for the Russians (or extramarital affairs for the French)—a game they know how to win. The middle class felt at ease when people could vote in free and fair elections, which were highly effective at assembling social coalitions and promoting middle-class interests and values. We have thus learned to expect that when the middle class takes to the streets (not a customary thing), it demands free and fair elections.

Yet recent event lead us to wonder whether the middle class's affection for elections might be waning. Russia, Thailand, and Turkey present three different and interesting cases. All three countries were shaken by mass political protests that cannot be explained away by the effects of the Great Recession. All three sailed reasonably well through the crisis, and they each represent different political regimes. On one level, this appears to confirm Fukuyama's thesis about the protests being led by a new global middle class that wants more participation and accountability with both democratic and nondemocratic regimes. But on another level, the three cases imply very different things about democracy, elections, and the political influence of the middle class.

In Russia in December 2011, the middle class took to the streets demanding free and fair elections—although one could bet that if they were free and fair, the middle class would have lost fair and square. In Thailand, the middle class protested for more than three months demanding "no elections," at least not in the next two years. (They insisted on an "appointed committee" to fix Thai politics and trumpeted the slogans "Reform before Election.") In Turkey, the situation was more confusing. Protesters were far-reaching in their criticism of the prime minister and called for the resignation of the government, but early parliamentary elections were not on their list of demands.

Why were the demands of the middle class so divergent in these three cases? Are we witnessing the political ascendance of a new middle class—or, alternatively, its political decline?

Russia

Alexei Slapovsky's 2010 novel *March on the Kremlin* opens with a young poet accidentally killed by a policeman. Not knowing whom to blame and what to do, the poet's mother picks up the body, cradles her dead son in her arms, and walks almost unconsciously toward the Kremlin. Her son's friends and several strangers trail close behind. Alerted via social media that something is happening, other people start to arrive.

Most of them are not really sure why they came out onto the streets. They do not have a common platform, common dream, or common leader; yet they are held together by a conviction that "enough is enough" and excited by the fact that at last something is happening. The Special Forces fail to stop them. The march suddenly reaches the Kremlin. And then . . . the people go back home.[8]

The nonfiction version of these events unfolded in Russia in December 2011. Moscow saw its largest protests since 1993. Though it was manipulated elections, not a poet's death, that sparked the crowd's anger, the protesters had one important element in common with the disaffected marchers in Slapovsky's novel: they seemed to emerge out of nowhere, taking almost everyone—including, perhaps, themselves—by surprise. The protesters were composed of an almost unimaginable crowd of liberals, nationalists, and leftists who had likely never spoken to each other and who for a few dizzying weeks dared to begin to imagine life without Putin.

Asked if the Kremlin was surprised by the unfolding of events, the senior United Russia functionary Yuri Kotler had been unambiguous: "Well, imagine if your cat came to you and started talking. First of all, it's a cat, and it's talking. Second, all these years, the government fed it, gave it water, petted it, and now it's talking and demanding something. It's a shock."[9]

Like most of the other recent eruptions of protest, the Russian Spring, in the dead of winter, did indeed come as a total shock. Few observers would have predicted Moscow's political turmoil. The Russian population has benefited economically from Putin's decade at the helm. Although the regime is corrupt and inefficient, it is reasonable to conclude that Russians have never been freer and wealthier in their history. Russia was a classic example of Hirschman's insight that in authoritarian regimes with open borders, the exit is a more likely choice than voice. Russia's dissatisfied middle class during the Putin years headed out to the airport and not to oppositional rallies.

In hindsight, one might suggest that the explosion of protest in Russia was simultaneously inevitable and impossible. It was born out of a sense of hurt pride, not deteriorating standards of living. Protesters were irate at the brazen, shameless way that President Medvedev and Prime Minister Putin privately decided to swap their positions. Of course, no one assumed Putin would step aside gracefully, but the public was humiliated by the fact that he did not even pretend that their opinion mattered at all.

In this sense, Russia's protests fit snugly with Fuku-yama's idea of a revolution of the global middle class. "It is a simple thing really," explains Ilya Faybisovich, one of the activists and protests organizers. "Before there had not been enough people who had enough to eat to care where the country was going; but now there are enough people who have enough to eat to care about the country in which their children will live." "What we saw in Bolotnaya Square," wrote independent journalists Andrei Soldatov and Irina Borogan, "was the Moscow middle class, made up of people who are well off, mostly educated, who spend a lot of time on the internet, and own a Mazda, Ford, or Nissan . . . More like a people at a cinema or a hyper-market than inspired revolutionaries."[10] It should also be stressed that this was not simply any middle class; it was Putin's middle class, the people who until yesterday were viewed as the biggest winners from Putin's time in power.

Russia's protest also aligns with the notion of a *social media revolution*. It was social networks, after all, that facilitated people taking to the streets for what were billed as major political discussions. But the Moscow protests also explain one less examined aspect of social networks—namely, their capacity to generate a "major-ity effect," the superficial sense that "everybody" is on our side, with "everybody" amounting to Facebook friends. It was social media that created the illusion that there is an anti-Putin majority in Russia. Revolutions often happen not because revolutionaries interpreted the situation cor-rectly, but because they got the situation wrong and then things happened to go right by chance.

During the long Putin decade, political theorists per-sistently wondered why people were not taking to the streets. Is it because Putin's majority is in fact real? Or is it because people are simply unaware of the emergence of an anti-Putin movement? The assumptions undergirding much democratic political theory suggest that people will readily protest if they know that the majority of citizens share their sentiments. A majority, even a vast one, may want change. But when each actor weighs the benefits of acting up against the dangers of being punished for doing so, most stay silent. A citizen will not risk danger unless he is convinced that he is part of the majority and that others will follow along.

In a similar way, authoritarian elites survive not when they are actually popular but when people *believe* that they are popular. Not surprisingly, control of the major television channels is at the heart of the Kremlin's managed democracy. In order for a protest to go viral, it is not sufficient that dissidents and "troublemakers" take to the streets. Citizens will join mass protests not when they see many people on the street, but when they see people they do not expect to be taking part in the unrest. This is precisely what happened in Moscow. Many of those on Bolotnaya Square and Sakharov Prospect were people you would not expect to find there bankers, former ministers, television celebrities, and fashion models. Putin's regime was not simply corrupt and inefficient. It became downright unfashionable even for its own elites. For a time, it was no longer hip to be pro-Putin in Moscow. It was also critically important that all the rallies were sanctioned by the authorities and that prior May 6, 2012, the day of President Putin's inauguration, the police were quite restrained in their actions.

The composition of the crowds on the street also explains the initial shock to those in power. Everyone knows that Russia's Special Forces are quite well trained to deal with rioting crowds. What they are not trained in, however, is how to contend with rioting elites. The Moscow protests also fit the pattern of the movement of the mistrustful. Russians flooded the streets but they did so without evincing any trust in anything or anybody. They loathed the leaders of the legal opposition (the Communists and the Just Russia party) and they had doubts about the traditional leaders of the more radical opposition (nonregistered parties). In short, the protesters suspected anybody who was an actual or wannabe politician.

What the Russian middle class wanted was representation that can challenge Putin's claim that he is Russia's one and only representative. The protesters looked to the Internet to compensate for the trust deficit. Secret online voting determined who would speak at rallies. The Internet was also the medium through which funds for the protests were collected. Ultimately, mistrust was both the movement's strength and its Achilles' heel. Moscow's middle class refused to be cheated, but they were also unwilling to be led. They were on the street to express their indignation about Putin and his regime but not to claim power. The protests waned almost immediately after the most popular opposition leader, Alexei Navalny, shouted that the demonstrators on the streets were the *people* and that power belonged to them.

In the months following the protests, there was much talk about why they remained confined to Moscow and a few other large cities. That question is no doubt relevant, but there are two others concerns at the heart of the Russian unrest. First, why were people so outraged about the government rigging elections? After all, Putin had rigged them before and always in an open and shameless manner. What was so different this time around? Second, and no less mysteriously, why did the protesters make free and fair elections their key demand when they were unable to agree on a common platform or leader, and when it was well understood that even if free and fair elections were held, Putin would prove victorious?

In his twelve-year rule, Putin has fashioned a political regime in which the elections are both meaningless and indispensable. That elections are "engineered," Julia Ioffe remarks, is "something everyone in Russia, no matter what their rhetoric or political persuasion, knows and accepts."[11] The dubious invalidation of signatures and disqualification of candidates, the stuffing of ballot boxes, the miscounting of votes, a monopoly on media, smear campaigns—these have long been staples of Russian elections.

For a decade now, most Russians have known that when it comes to elections, the fix is in. And most have also believed that had the electoral process been free and fair Putin would have come out on top anyway. Even when labeling Putin "the most sinister figure in contemporary Russian history," a leading spokesman for the Russian human rights movement reluctantly admitted some years ago that "Putin would have won the campaigns of 2000 and 2004—though perhaps without such large, unseemly margins—even if they had been free of vote tampering and the illegal use of the government's so-called 'administrative resources,' and if the candidates had actually had equal access to the voters through television and the press."[12]

In an essay penned with the American political theorist Stephen Holmes, I have argued that rigged elections that fail to be broadly decried illustrate the real source of legitimacy of Putin's regime. Election rigging is less an imitation of democracy, per se, than it is the best way to prove the government's authoritarian street credibility without resorting to mass repression. Swallowed by the public, rigged elections send a message that the government is in control and nothing will change.

Seen in this light, Russian protesters were not expecting elections they could win, or even elections in which they could compete. They were simply demanding the end of Putin's version of "no alternative" politics. The alternative to Putin was endorsed irrespective of who or what it was. Indeed, after the first two weeks of euphoria, the protesters well understood they were not speaking for the majority of Russians. But what they did demonstrate was the existence of a sizable anti-Putin minority. It is the right to be represented as a minority that explains Moscow's middle class's attitude toward politicians of the opposition: they do not like them much, they do not trust them much, and they could not see them as future leaders. That said, they were grateful of their existence. Unlike their Bulgarian cousins who wanted elections but were not ready to take part in them, Russians wanted elections so they can freely vote for anybody who was not Putin.

The ideological diversity of the protesters gave them a sense that they might speak on behalf of Russia. In one sense, this represented a real achievement. The spectacular ascension of the anticorruption blogger Alexei Navalny and a general recognition of an anti-Putin minority were more concrete successes. The protests eventually ended with regime change of a sort. Putin's politics of no alternatives was smashed. The demand for free and fair elections, even in its twisted logic, touched on the third rail of the regime's ideology—the absence of alternative futures. The Kremlin's message of "Putin for Life" would now be interpreted to mean "no life after Putin."

The Russian protests demonstrate the limitations of elections as an instrument for legitimizing nondemocratic regimes. While in democracies elections regulate society by creating drama, Russia's elections without choice function as terminators of the future. Authoritarian regimes bet that the future will resemble the past, and the major demand of protesters in Russia was the demand for leaving the future open.

In the end, Russia's middle class—while not producing any realistic alternative to power—did usher in a change, just not the one for which the protesters hoped. Before December 2011, President Putin governed as if there was a Putin consensus, and on behalf of the nation as a whole. Following the protests, his strategy of cooptation was replaced by confrontation. Putin was forced to govern solely on behalf of his majority. The protest pushed Putin to confront the truth revealed by Berthold Brecht some seventy years ago during Berlin uprising of 1953: that if he was unhappy with the people, his only choice was to elect a new one. This is what Putin effectively did by dismissing those protesting against him as gays, lesbians, and foreign agents. Anyone who rejected him was automatically excommunicated from the ranks of the Russian people. Russia's annexation of Crimea was the last act in the post-protest transformation of Putin's regime. What started as "Occupy Abay" ended as "Occupy Crimea."

Thailand

"It was all wearily familiar," the BBC correspondent Jonathan Head noted on the third month of antigovernment protests in Thailand. "The shrieking whistles, the colorful umbrellas, the rousing speeches, and music from the stages." But this color-coded political conflict in Thailand was different from the other middle-class protests. It began in November 2013 and brought 100,000 people to the streets after Thailand's lower house passed an amnesty bill, which critics said could allow the former Prime Minister Shinawatra Thaksin (now self-exiled in London) to return to the country without serving time in jail for a corruption conviction. The Senate later rejected the bill, but the demonstrators refused to go home. The Thai protest is not easy to interpret in the context of the revolution of the global middle class; it is simply the last of a series of protests and counterprotests that have shattered Thailand since 2006. Much more significantly, it contradicts the general claim that the last wave of middle-class protests represents the middle class's commitment to democracy.

Protesters on the streets of Bangkok, unified in their hatred of Prime Minister Yingluck Shinawatra and her family (she is Thaksin's sister), were not necessarily demanding elections, but rather the postponement of elections in general for two years. Many speculate that the real purpose of the protest was to provoke the army to take power. That said, protesters did everything possible to prevent the February 2 elections and succeeded in blocking them in some electoral districts while failing to prevent the majority of people from voting.

Why in the Thai case did the middle class turn against elections? How significant is this surprising turn?

Although the middle class supported the exiled former Prime Minister Thaksin Shinawatra in the 2001 and 2005 elections, by 2006 it had turned against him. Critics accused Thaksin of manipulating government policy to favor his business interests, implementing irresponsible populist policies and undermining the legitimacy of the old elite. The middle class felt trapped because the Thaksin Shinawatra government (2001–2006) and the current Yingluck Shinawatra government have threatened it by championing redistributive programs and by establishing an unbeatable coalition between the richest family in the country and the rural and urban poor. In their view, Thaksin's camp was "buying the vote" with irresponsible economic policies and, while in power, "selling" its private assets at a higher-than-market price.

The problem for the demonstrators is that the government's support among the rural poor gives the Shinawatra coalition a virtually unassailable majority—hence its opponents' blunt rebuff of democratic principles: "Lack of trust, empathy, and denial of reality seem to pervade Thai society," wrote the daily newspaper the *Nation*.

While the Thai protests are quite culturally specific and burdened with local history, they nevertheless point to a critical question evident in many of the recent middle-class protests. Why is the middle class more and more seen protesting on the streets? Is it an expression of a pent-up demand for new and higher standards of transparency and accountability? Is it an expression of its new power? Or, alternatively, is it a sign of the isolation and decline of the political influence of the global middle class in electoral politics generally?

Of course, it would not be the first time that the middle class opposed the demands of the poorer groups in society. What is new, however, is that—at least as I write—the middle class is losing its capacity to form political coalitions and to use formal democratic institutions (including elections) to advance its own interests.

The protests demonstrate that unlike the national bourgeoisies, the global middle class has lost its capacity to make social coalitions. This could be easily witnessed not only in Thailand but also in Russia, Turkey, and Bulgaria. At the very moment the middle class has lost its interest in governing, others have lost interest in the middle class itself. Not coincidentally, the protests have had real difficulty spreading outside the capitals and large cities. Indeed, it is the very libertarian nature of the new global middle class that has left it in isolation. While the new middle class was losing interest in the state, both the oligarchs and the poor were betting on it. What Fukuyama sees as a revolution of the global middle class is in fact an uprising of the global middle-class *individual*—that is, more powerful than his predecessors but less capable of collective action, and above all incapable of finding public figures to represent its interests.

The new middle-class individual—armed with an iPhone and living in a world of global comparisons—has trouble finding allies at home. The international media lavishes praise on him, he dominates the social networks, and he is able to connect with people like him across national borders. But he is patently hamstrung when it comes to forming social connections with the poor and uneducated in his own society.

But what the middle class lost at the ballot box cannot be compensated for in the streets, principally because of the middle class's incapacity to bring about genuine disruption. In a way, it is a mark of self-preservation or middle-class status to go and protest on the street; it is also part of the same status logic not to stay in the street for too long, since only professional revolutionaries, the unemployed, or radicals interested in fomenting violence can afford to do that. The defenders of the current protests have been particularly encouraged by their anarchist soul—no leaders, no parties, no programs. But the middle class remains instinctively averse to disorder. Its members can play at revolution, but they cannot tolerate chaos. This is one reason the governments, which made it their strategy to discredit and exhaust the protests rather than crush them, were successful at keeping people power.

Since 2006, mass political protests in Thailand—first by anti-Thaksin "yellow shirts" and later by pro-Thaksin "red shirts"—have in practice determined who will govern the country. In this way, mass political protests were not complementary to electoral democracy but an alternative to it. The middle class lost hope that they could be successful at the ballot box.

The paradox in all this is that the spread of democracy has weakened the political power of the social group traditionally viewed as democracy's social base. The middle classes are less prepared to win elections, as the Thailand case makes clear, and have lost all hope for success against a coalition of the oligarchs and the poor. But when they have taken to the streets, middle-class protesters lack the radicalism that minorities committed to street politics desperately need if they hope to succeed.

Turkey

"One finds peace in revolt" reads one of the thousands of graffiti slogans that blanketed Istanbul during the summer of 2013. Turkey certainly seemed the unlikeliest candidate for a popular uprising. It had one of Europe's few thriving economies, with record economic growth, falling unemployment, and decreasing urban poverty. Turks have never been better educated and freer in their history. It was a society seemingly full of optimism, with the average age under thirty and half the population under twenty-five. In a period of widely unpopular governments all over Europe, Turkey's was genuinely supported. In three consecutive parliamentary elections since 2002, the governing AKP of Prime Minister Recep Tayyip Erdoğan not only won but increased its margin of victory each time.

Turkey, however, saw one of the most spectacular political protests of 2013. It all began on May 28 in Istanbul, when a group of environmentalists and local activists occupied Gezi Park in opposition to a plan to build a shopping mall on one of the few major parks left in the sprawling urban metropolis that is Istanbul—a city of more than 13 million people. What started out as a protest by a few people grew quickly into a nationwide crisis after images circulated on social media sites of the repressive approach taken by the police toward the protesters. Pictures of fully armored riot police spraying tear gas provoked indignation and disgust. According to a report by the ministry of the interior, a total of 3,545,000 citizens participated in 4,725 events in all but one of Turkey's eighty-one provinces.

The protests brought together individuals convinced that Prime Minister Erdoğan is guilty of increasing authoritarianism and attempting to force his will on Turkish society. Not unlike Charles de Gaulle during the events of May 1968, Erdoğan has become the symbol of a great national leader who has outlived his usefulness. The public was infuriated by his desire to dictate a dress code for the country's popular soap operas and by his attempt to control the media and pressure critical voices on television and in the newspapers. The final straw was provoked by new government regulations restricting the sale of alcohol and banning all images, advertisements, and movie scenes that promote alcohol consumption.

Although Turkey's democracy has been regularly praised for its success in reconciling the secular nature of the state with the Islamic roots of the governing party, the protests unveiled another face of Turkish democracy. Television stations somehow "forgot" to observe the protests; their coverage of the events was even worse than what the Putin-controlled media managed during the protests in Russia. And the police went overboard in the use of force and in highly ineffective and counterproductive techniques of crowd control. The disproportionate force deployed by the police ended up killing five protesters, blinding eleven, and leaving thousands injured. Erdoğan may have been a good father to the Turks, but in the summer of 2013 it became evident that the children felt they had reached the age of maturity.

What makes the Turkish protests central to the discussion is the extraordinary mixture of people and ideologies

on the streets. Turkey had seen large anti-Erdoğan rallies before. In 2007, the old Kemalist elite organized mass
demonstrations against the election of Erdoğan as president. Turkey was also no stranger to leftist and anticapitalist riots. What was different this time, however, was the
spontaneous and leaderless nature of the protests, and the
fact that protesters were representing political groups that
had not previously assembled. One saw secularists protesting against the Islamist government as well as leftist
groups militating against the capture of public spaces by
the private sector. People with contrasting political views
and separate agendas not only came together in protest
but also succeeded in developing a common language.

In this sense, what happened in Taksim Square was
quite unlike Moscow's protest. In Russia, liberals, leftists,
and nationalists found a common cause in a common
enemy (Putin); in Turkey, the protesters constructed a
common conversation. The rejection of Erdoğan's political style was accompanied by serious criticism of the
major opposition parties and the way political representation has historically operated in Turkey. One of the banners
read: "We are not a political party, we are the people." In
Taksim Square, supporters of the three prominent football
teams in Turkey—Fenerbahçe, Galatasaray, and Beşiktaş—
stood together *for the first time ever.* "The demonstrations,"
claimed the leading Turkish analyst Soli Ozel, "transformed
Turkey in ways that are both visible and not immediately
penetratable [*sic*]. The urban populations escaped the
desperation caused by the absence of a viable democratic
alternative on the political scene."[13]

The Turkish protesters called for Erdoğan's resignation, but they did not make early elections a key demand.

Their ambition was not to topple the AKP but to draw a fixed line that no politician from any party should ever cross. The protesters knew that Erdoğan had won elections that were free and fair. Some of them had even voted for the AKP; others were ready to vote for it again. What united everyone, ultimately, was the conviction that in a democracy electoral success does not permit you to interfere with the personal lifestyles of the people.

Democracy without Elections

In his dispatches from the Indignados' "revolution of soul," *La Vanguardia* reporter Andy Robinson observed that "Madrid's iconic central square, La Puerta del Sol, was the site of a strange convergence between the cyber age and the Middle Ages." It was not simply because Spanish Indignados claimed protection under a decree that secures the right of shepherds to camp with their flocks on ancient grazing routes, but because the twenty-first-century protests resemble, in some respects, the protests of the medieval period. In the Middle Ages, people went to the streets without the ambition of overthrowing the king or putting a new king on the throne. They took to the streets to force those ruling to do something for their well-being, or to prevent them from doing something harmful.

In his remarkable book *Counter-Democracy*, French political philosopher Pierre Rosanvallon best captures the simultaneously pre- and postpolitical nature of the new generation of civic activism. Rosanvallon anticipated the emergence of leaderless protest as an instrument for transforming democracy in the twenty-first century. Accepting the reality of a democracy of mistrust, he does not go on to suggest that what we are experiencing today is a crisis that will be inevitably overcome, where trust in institutions and leaders will be restored to their rightful place. According to Rosanvallon, democracy will now inevitably be a way of organizing the all-pervasive mistrust that surrounds us in all directions. In fact, Rosanvallon believes that mistrust has been at the heart of the democratic project from the beginning. "Distrust . . . is . . . to liberty what jealousy is to love," claimed the unsentimental Robespierre more than two centuries ago.

In this, a world defined by mistrust, popular sovereignty will assert itself as the power to refuse. Do not expect politicians with long-range visions or political movements to inspire collective projects. Do not expect political parties to capture the imagination of the citizens and command the loyalty of their followers. The democracy of the future will look very different. People will step into the civic limelight only to refuse certain policies or debunk particular politicians. The core social conflicts that will structure political space will be between the people and the elite, not between left and right. The democracy of tomorrow—being born today on the streets of the world's great cities—will be a democracy of rejection.

The protesters on the streets of Moscow, Sofia, Istanbul, and São Paulo are the new face of democratic politics. But please do not ask them what they want. What they know is only what they do not want. Their rejectionist ethic may be as radical and total as dismissing world capitalism (see Occupy Wall Street) or as local and modest as a protest against a new railway station in Stuttgart. But the principle is the same. We do not make positive choices anymore; we are active in politics by our readiness to reject. Protests may succeed or fail, but what defines their politics is an all-embracing *no*, and to vocalize it, one no longer needs leaders or institutions; social networks and smartphones will suffice.

We are heading to a new democratic age in which politicians will not have our trust and citizens will be preoccupied with controlling their representatives. Political representation does not work in an era inhabited by people with multiple identities. "Why should it be more important for me that I am German than that I am a cyclist," a young member of the European parliament from the Greens told me. She refused to think in terms of social or ethnic groups and she refused to take history into account. Nothing should constrain or challenge the freedom of her individual choices.

In the new democratic age, electoral politics will no longer take pride of place. Elections have lost their connection to the future. "Tomorrow never happens. It is the same fucking day, man," sings Janis Joplin. We might label it "the Chinese turn," as it is they who believe that what stands in front of us is the past, not the future. Elections today are a judgment about the past, not a gamble on what is coming next. Until recently, voting was about choosing a government as well as a policy. But contemporary elections are really only about selecting governors, the "managers of the present." Voters have decoupled policy makers from policies. When you fail to believe that the government actually makes a difference on economic matters or foreign policy, what counts is not the new ideas a politician might implement down the road but their capacity to keep things from getting worse.

The new democratic citizen is tired of voting for governments without qualities. When it comes to addressing social problems, the "new political man" might choose between taking the government to court, launching an NGO, or joining some ad hoc initiative designed to improve the world. When he has the sense that some basic democratic rights are being violated, he can take to the street or use his Facebook page to mobilize mass protest— and we should not be surprised if thousands show up.

What makes the new democratic age so different is the profound primacy placed on the individual. The individual decides whether to sue the government or not. The individual, deprived of any social qualities or organizational connections, occupies the squares. The new political man has no illusions about the ineffectiveness of government but he believes that people have a responsibility to control it. The passion for transparency and the obsession with accountability are a natural reaction to the loss of representation. Civic participation is no longer about power—it is about influence. The new movements of mistrust are better suited than traditional revolutionary movements for an age in which, as Rosanvallon puts it, "the goal of politics is more to *deal with situations* than to organize stable groups and manage hierarchical structures."[14]

If we trust Rosanvallon, *the watcher* and not the voter is becoming the critical figure in democratic politics. But if Calvino's watcher was responsible for the fairness of the electoral process and for guaranteeing that people will be fairly and accurately represented, the new watchers are in the business of observing those already in power. Elections are losing their central role; instead we are left with three different modes of political activism. On the individual level, any time we believe our rights are violated we can sue the government. We can also promote certain issues and policies through NGOs and other forms of ad hoc civic activism (and to do so we do not need to be members of political parties or even to vote). Then there is the symbolic level of politics—when we want to raise hell and shock the system. At these times, we can take to the streets. What is missing in this vision of political activism is the idea of loyalty. Hirschman's opposition between exit and voice assumed that the citizen, unlike the consumer, was bound by national and civic loyalties. But in our new democratic world, loyalty has evaporated. Politics has been replaced by collective consumerism in which citizens regularly appeared poised to bolt for the door.

Chapter 3

Exit Politics

I can only love what I am free to leave

—Wolf Biermann,
Poems and Ballads

Inspired by the East Germans' triumph over communism by leaving rather than fighting, several West German anarchists in 1990 designed a monument, *Unknown Deserters*, commemorating those who perished in both world wars: "This is for the man who refused to kill his fellow man," the monument read, a silhouette of a running man carved into a block of granite. Anarchists, who carried it from city square to city square, hoped East Germans would countenance defection as a form of class struggle and embrace the concept of a one-person revolution. You do not need parties or revolutionary armies to change the world, the anarchists' radical message seemed to say; it is enough that individuals leave the country when asked to violate their principles. The current wave of protests shares with the East German exodus of 1989 this explicit refusal to get sullied by the game of international politics.

At the same time that the *Unknown Deserters* monument was on tour across East Germany, seventy-year-old Albert O. Hirschman was ensconced as a visiting fellow in the *Wissenschaftskolleg,* the Institute for Advanced Studies in Berlin. The collapse of the German Democratic Republic (GDR) provoked him to rethink the complex and fraught relationship between his master concepts of exit and voice. The existence of the two German states was a remarkable historical experiment in which *migrating* Germans magically adjusted his conception of *exit.* Hirschman set out to understand what happened in that annus mirabilis of 1989 and how the inexorable seesaw of exit and voice could have "suddenly turned into a joint grave-digging act."[1]

In Hirschman's analysis, the regime's coda was an outcome both of the failure of the communist government to prevent exit after the erection of the Berlin Wall and of the decision to ignore the political importance of mass exits in the summer of 1989. It was during this hot summer that it became clear that those who were disloyal to the GDR were working hard to leave the country, while those who retained faith were incensed by their government's unspoken support for the emigration of these undesirables. Rather than precluding the voice option, the mass migration of the summer of 1989 mobilized it. When citizens took to the streets, it was thus hardly surprising that they demanded two things: free elections (voice) and free travel (exit).

There is a similar illustration of this exit-voice logic in many of the recent protests we have been discussing. The citizen who decides to leave the country hardly has reform in mind. He is interested in changing his own lot in life, not the lives of others. But the use of exit by governments as a way to reduce the pressure for change can be an impetus for bringing protesters to the streets. The impact of the global financial crisis on the growth of protest politics was most strongly felt not through the rise unemployment and economic hardship, but through the evaporation of emigration as an option to deal with social and economic pressures. The crisis was global. There was nowhere people could go to escape. Imagine West Germany suddenly disappearing in 1989.

In the last few decades, mobility has been a major characteristic of the global middle class. Middle-class individuals have been empowered by the freedom to leave. The financial crisis reversed this perspective, however, and exit began to be perceived as a sign of disempowerment. In order to understand the logic of the current protest wave in the world, particularly in Europe, we need to grasp this redefinition of voice and exit. In places like Russia and Bulgaria, protesters conceptualize their street demonstrations as a rejection of exit. "We are on the streets," protesters commonly say, "because we don't want to emigrate. If the protest fails, however, we will."[2] Yet in their organizational logic, the protests can in fact be interpreted as a collective act of exit; the protesters reject representation and the possibility to negotiation and even agreement on a common platform or list of demands. But by denying the state of normal politics organized around conflicts between organized social groups, the protesters have been forced to oscillate between the individual and symbolic level of politics. They have had to choose between being either wholly concrete or deeply abstract in their demands.

In 2011, *Adbusters* magazine released the now famous poster in which a ballerina danced over the symbolic bull of the New York Stock Exchange, calling on activists to occupy Wall Street. At the top of the poster, one reads the line: "What is our one demand?" In a democracy without representation, all political movements have the right of a single demand. It might be very concrete—say, lowering the bus fare in San Paolo or dispensing with plans to rebuild the Stuttgart railway station. In such cases, there is a fair chance that the demand will be met. Or the demand can be grandiose and symbolic, as in ending capitalism, and then the meaning becomes the demand itself. In order for the protest to be successful, it should be either concrete or symbolic. The middle level—messy space of actual politics that cannot be addressed by crowds huddled in public squares—has disappeared.

In many respects, the current revolt against political representation resembles the situation in ancient Rome, when plebs (Rome's middle class) decided to leave the city, separate themselves, "go away," and thus demonstrate their collective rejection of the status quo. Beginning 453 BC, the plebs would occasionally exit the city, evacuating Rome and encamping on one of the neighboring hills as an explicit expression of their civic anger. "They are without any leader," wrote Titus Livy, the great chronicler of ancient Rome, "their camp being fortified with a rampart and trench, remaining quiet, taking nothing but what was necessary for sustenance, they kept themselves for several days, neither being attacked, nor attacking others. Great was the panic in the city, and through mutual fear all was suspense. The people left in the city dreaded the violence of the senators; the senators dreaded the people remaining in the city, uncertain whether they should prefer them to stay or to depart; but how long would the multitude, which has seceded, remain quiet? What were to be the consequences then, if in the meantime, any foreign war should break out?"[3]

This secession was nothing more than an appeal for the refounding of the political community around principles dear to its rebellious citizens. As Livy indicates, the plebs agreed to return to the city only when the senators succeeded in fashioning a narrative that recognized the plebs' significance to society as well as their power. The institution of the tribunes—the ones who have the power to veto the decisions of the senate—was born out of the secessions. Secessions were different from conspiracies and civil wars. They were not about changing those who govern. They were about the principles according to which power is exercised. In a society that believed in the cyclical nature of history and where the future was simply another name for the past, they were truly revolutionary. The secessions did not hope to bring change; they demanded the restoration of cosmic order.

Today's mass protests, in many respects, are acts in search of a concept; they are praxis, if you will, without theory. They are the most dramatic expression of the conviction that the elites do not govern in the interest of the people and that the electorate has lost control over the elected. They stand for an insurrection against the institutions of representative democracy but without offering any alternatives (or even an openness to endorse non-democratic replacements). This new wave of protests is leaderless not because social media made leaderless revolutions possible (last we checked ancient Rome was not wired), but because the ambition to challenge all forms of political representation has made political leaders unwelcome.

In my previous book, *In Mistrust We Trust*, I argued that while globalization has empowered the middle-class individual, it has disempowered the voter. Once upon a time, a voter's power derived from the fact that he was a citizen-soldier, a citizen-worker, and/or a citizen-consumer. The *citizen-soldier* was important because the defense of the country depended on his courage to stand against his enemies. The *citizen-worker* was significant because his labor made the country rich, and the *citizen-consumer* mattered because his consumption drove the economy. But globalization liberated the elites from their dependence on citizens. When drones and professional armies replace the citizen-soldier, elites lose interest in the views of citizen-soldiers. The flooding of the labor market by low-cost immigrants or outsourced production reduces the elites' willingness to cooperate. As a result, the citizen-worker gets detached from the citizen-voter.[4]

During the recent economic crisis, it became evident that the performance of the American stock market no longer depended on American consumerism. The *general strike* had lost its political power. At the same time, elections fail to evince either the drama or the capacity to solve social problems that they once did, while rebellion from below has become unconvincing. Capturing the government is simply no longer a guarantee that things will change. Voter power is constrained today not just because the voter has lost his additional capacities that derive from his other social roles and participation in stable social groups but also because the voter does not know whom to blame for his misfortunes. The more transparent our societies become, the more difficult it is for citizens to decide where to direct their anger. We live in a society of "innocent criminals," where governments prefer to claim impotence rather than power.

In her classic mystery *Murder on the Orient Express*, Agatha Christie tells the story of a very unusual murder in which all twelve suspects are guilty of committing a crime, and the police are forced to either acknowledge it or pretend that a stranger who exited the train is the culprit. Our angry citizen finds himself in a similar dilemma. He is angry at power but he does not know who to blame— those in government, those behind the government, the very idea of a government, the market, Brussels (for those who are EU members), and so forth. If a citizen today seeks to criticize, say, rising inequality, to what should he turn to find those responsible? The market? The government? New technologies? Could any government succeed in reducing inequality on its own without destroying his country's competitiveness? The futile attempts of several leftist governments to increase taxes on the superrich are the most powerful demonstration of the constraints that governments face in an era of global markets and international capital flow. It is unclear if it would make more sense to topple the government or pity it.

Voters feel helpless today because the politicians they choose are candid about their lack of power. It is up to citizens to decide whether to trust that the politicians do in fact have their hands tied or to treat the cries of powerlessness as the ultimate power grab. "I am tired of austerity, I want promises," reads a graffiti in Brazil. The author of the outcry captures something fundamental. In a democratic politics without alternatives, politicians make a virtue out of promising nothing. But a stance of "no promises" translates to even less power for the voters. Democracy is nurtured by promises because politicians who fail to fulfill them can be held accountable. When there are no promises, there is no civic responsibility. "I didn't promise you anything" is a line out of a cheap romance novel. After hearing it, the only thing the jilted lover can do is run away and cry.

It is through this prism that we can apprehend the meaning of the wave of protests that have rocked the world in recent years. The prism also enables us to ponder the political changes they may bring. The protests are a rejection of a politics without possibility, but they are also a form of acceptance of this new reality. None of the protest movements emerged with a platform for changing the world, or even the economy. In this sense, they are not Paul Mason's anticapitalist revolution. In fact, they might be seen as capitalism's safety valve. Karl Marx would probably tell today's rebels that anticapitalist protest is essential for the relegitimation of global capitalism.

Neither are the protests examples of Fukuyama's revolution of the global middle class—at least not in the sense of them being a demonstration of its empowerment. After all, it was during these protests that the middle class proved its own loss of political strength. But if the protests do not signal a return of revolutionary politics, neither will they represent an effective strategy of citizen empowerment in the age of globalization. Where governments are less powerful than before, corporations are more mobile, and political parties bereft of the capacity to build a political identity around visions for the future, the power of citizens derives from their ability to disrupt.

Democracy by Other Means

Protests, unlike elections, are unexpected. It is their anti-institutional ethos that makes them what they are. If protests are a rotten instrument for governing, they are a great tool for controlling government. The form of control is, however, very different from the form embodied in elections. In electoral politics, we control politicians by determining whether they represent the voters by keeping their promises. The notion of control in protest politics is instead focused on manipulating the elites to prevent them from benefiting from their positions of power. It is the protests' spontaneity that makes it difficult for the elites to capture them. In different environments, protests will have varying objectives and social compositions, but what is common in all of them tends to be a reaction to a state and economy captured by special interests. In the examples of Bulgaria, Turkey, and many of the other countries in turmoil, those who control executive power are also those who dominate judicial power: standard separation of powers does not apply and mass protests remain the only effective way to resist institutional capture and to force a fissure within the elite. In this sense, the rise of protest politics is a natural outcome of the oligarchic turn in democratic politics.

The current protest wave has transformed democratic politics. These days they serve as a kind of democratic stress test for governments. In fact, the capacity to deal with protests rather than the capacity to win elections is what distinguishes democratic governments from nondemocratic ones. In the United States and Spain, governments were quick to recognize the legitimacy of the protesters' concerns and to signal that those grievances were being heard. Protests did not change what governments were actually doing but rather how they spoke about what they were doing. We now see that democratic governments are able to exhaust protest movements while nondemocratic governments (even when democratically elected) try to crash them.

Most striking about the current protest wave has been less the way protesters in different corners of the world have mimicked each other, but rather the nearly identical response of governments we view as fundamentally different. In places like Russia, Turkey, and Ukraine, it was as if the responses emanated from a common script. If the protests were well organized, they were passed off and discredited as "unspontaneous." As for the conspiracy theories, it was as if they had been fashioned collaboratively. Erdoğan blamed the protests on the interest-rates lobby in Turkey; Putin on foreign agents underwritten by the American embassy; the Ukrainian government on extreme nationalists and certain oligarchs manipulated by the West. In all these countries, foreign-funded NGOs became the bogeymen, with George Soros playing the lead, supposedly directing everything behind the scenes.

As a rule, the police were deployed without any restraints. The message of the respective governments was not so much as "trust us"—most of them knew that this would be a fool's errand— but "do not trust anybody." This strategy succeeded in Russia, worked partially in Turkey, and backfired in Ukraine. Protests served the same role as police experiments in solving crimes. Responding to the protests, democratic governments are usually asked to prove their democratic credentials. (These days it is difficult to hold governments accountable for job creation, but they can be held responsible for the loss of life.) But it is their behavior in the face of mutiny that determines their legitimacy. Ukraine was the consummate example of a popularly elected president losing legitimacy because he chose a strategy of wiping out the protests.

The protests remind those in power of the limits of elite attempts to capture democratic institutions. While the protesters view elections as a mechanism of elite control over society, the protests themselves serve as people's surest instrument of controlling and checking the power of elites. Protests ruin the international reputation of a country and the domestic legitimacy of those in power. Because protesters are no longer sure who governs, they end up attacking the whole system of governance. Was it not symptomatic that protesters in the United States occupied Wall Street rather than the White House? Similarly, was it not curious to watch how Western politicians threatened to impose sanctions on Ukrainian oligarchs for the country's bloodshed even though those oligarchs were not directly in charge of the government? The oligarchs were not surprised because they were well aware of their own indirect power. Unlike elections, which focus only on direct, formal centers of power, protests promise to destroy the *real* centers of power—which are far more dispersed throughout the society, culture, and economy.

The power of protest is negative. It injects insecurity into the elite, and it is the contagious nature of protest that turns it into a global issue. Taking to the streets of their own cities, protesters accumulate enough power to be heard by the powers that be of the world over. Mass protests in small countries can have an impact that no election ever could.

Protests are also more effective than elections at triggering splits in the elite on both the national and international levels. Mass protests immediately divide the elite between those who want to engage and those who want to crush, between those who want to dialogue with the protesters and those who would rather arrest them. The protests also break elite solidarity on the international level. This is particularly true in EU member states. When in the summer of 2013 the German and French ambassadors in Sofia sided with the protesters against the legitimate government of a member state, they had a point. Nothing less than the legitimacy of the EU project as a citizen-led affair was at stake.

The protests are also designed to assert the subjectivity of the people at the very moment when they lack the opportunity to make big political choices. Even when they are not advocating anything concrete, the protests assert the possibility of change and thus do something that elections once did—keep the future open. People who occupy public spaces get a sense of power that is absent in the electoral booth. They also create community. People who take an active part in such protests customarily make them a part of their political identity. But those who take to the streets remember not their defeat but their sense of power. Mass protest immediately brings back memories of revolutions that succeeded in changing the status quo.

The most notable consequence of the current protest wave is that it has made protesting popular. A study of public attitudes in Russia a year after the protest movement's defeat demonstrates this best. Although political mobilization has declined in Moscow and other centers of protest activity, the numbers of those outside those centers (who previously opposed the demonstrations) who say they would rise up if their interests were threatened has doubled. In Bulgaria, the protest wave led to a decline in trust for all public institutions, while trust in democracy increased. That said, the protests leave the policy initiative with the same elites who held the reins of power before.

What, then, is the actual meaning of the protests? Are we witnessing "the continuation, at all costs, of a weary world? A salutary crisis of that world . . . ? The end of that world? The advent of a different world?"[5]

Regardless of the myriad demonstrations of civic courage and political idealism and the inspiring videos and rich expressions of countercultural imagination, the protests are not the solution to "there is no alternative" politics. They are, however, powerful manifestations of resistance to the subordination of politics to the market (even when they are promarket). In the final account, the protests demonstrate the resilience of the political but signal a decline of political reform. The waning of the voice option is a side effect of this new generation of political mobilization. In political activism that is so individualistic and symbolic, there is no place for Hirschman's small-scale reformers. Contemporary protests are therefore much more about exit than voice.

A number of commentators view the mass protests as a kind of nongovernmental revolution. In some respects they are right. Many of the protest activists were socialized in the NGO community, and their stress on transparency and control come straight from an NGO playbook. But the age of protest may also mark the twilight for NGOs—and they may become paradoxically the period's big losers. Indeed the anti-institutional message of the protests drives the younger generation toward spontaneous, Internet-centered activism and discourages more formal organizational thinking. Since many governments deny the spontaneous nature of the protests and seek to pin blame on a handful of masterminds, NGOs are an easy culprit. Not surprisingly, the protests inspired governments in several cases to introduce anti-NGO laws.

In investigating the mysterious murder of Professor Grimaud and the equally incredible killing on Cagliostro Street, the esteemed detective Dr. Fell in John Dickson Carr's mystery novel *The Three Coffins* learns a valuable lesson. When trying to solve a murder or figure out a magician's trick, you often find yourself looking at the clue without seeing it, or swearing you see it when there's really nothing there.

Applying Dr. Fell's method works well in unraveling the mystery of the latest eruption of popular protests. The protests have not marked the return of revolution. Like elections, they actually serve to forestall revolution by keeping its promise of a radically different future at an unbridgeable distance. "The graduate looking for work" is not the new proletarian. Revolutions need ideology as oxygen and fuel, and the protesters have no ideology or alternative vision of the future to speak of.

The protesters disrupt democracy, but then democracy returns, poised and primed for the next disruption. Which will come. And then end. Just like the last time. Just like the next.

A c k n o w l e d g m e n t s

The origins of small books—like the origins of mass protests—are always veiled in mystery. They are spontaneous and leaderless. They are born of collective emotions and collective experiences, so allow me to express my gratitude to those who took to the streets of Sofia on June 14, 2013, and to my colleagues from the Centre for Liberal Strategies in that same city, who helped me to experience from a distance the workings of these protests.

The book was written during the time I was a Richard von Weizsacker Fellow of the Bosch Foundation, so I am deeply grateful to Sandra Breka and her colleagues in the Bosch office in Berlin for their support. There was no better place to write this book.

My colleagues at the Institute for Human Sciences in Vienna, where I am a permanent fellow, have contributed in innumerable ways to my reflections on the protest experience. It was my luck that in the time of writing the book, I was able to discuss it with Marci Shore and Timothy Snyder. My colleague and friend Ilia Iliev was extremely helpful with his suggestions and criticism. Just as I was starting to reflect on the complex relations between protests and democracy, the institute's founding

Acknowledgments

rector Krzysztof Michalski passed away. He was an exceptional figure and I hope that this book manages to express at least some small amount of all I learned from him over the years.

As with my previous book, *In Mistrust We Trust*, Professor Stephen Holmes from New York University and Leonard Benardo from the Open Society Foundations are a sort of undercover coauthors. The book was written in a constant dialogue with them. Lenny not only simply lent me some of his ideas but was also the one who translated the first draft from "my English" into English. Maria Lipman, Soli Özel, and Jonas Rolett, Craig Kennedy, Marc Plattner, and Venelin Ganev were some of the people with whom I discussed my ideas as they were taking shape, and who took time to comment on the manuscript.

This book would never have been written if Mark Lilla had not suggested to Damon Linker of the University of Pennsylvania Press that I might have a book like this in me. It was Damon who took the risk of asking me to write it—and then took on the task of editing it. Working with him was a real privilege. I am grateful for his labors.

To my family I owe the greatest thanks. Dessy knows this book better than I do, as she was the first careful critical reader of every sentence in it. It was my daughter Niya who insisted I should see *Catching Fire* and introduced me to the world of *Hunger Games*. My five-year-old son, Yoto, contributed to the book not by editing or suggesting ideas but by constantly reminding me that writing books is not, after all, the most important thing.

N o t e s

Introduction

1. Alexis Tocqueville, *Recollections: The French Revolution of 1848* (Edison, New Jersey: Transaction, 1989), 30.

2. John B. Halstead, ed., *Contemporary Writings of the Coup d' État of Louis Napoleon* (New York: Doubleday, 1972).

3. Paul Mason, *Why It's Kicking Off Everywhere: The New Global Revolutions* (London: Verso, 2012), 45.

4. David Hume, *Essays: Moral, Political and Literary* (New York: Cosimo, 2006), 29.

5. Eric Schmidt and Jared Cohen, *The New Digital Age: Reshaping the Future of People, Nations and Business* (New York: Knopf, 2013).

Chapter 1: Protest Against Politics

1. Alain Badiou, *The Rebirth of History: Times of Riots and Uprisings*, trans. Gregory Elliott (New York: Verso, 2012).

2. The *Economist* Intelligence Unit, "Rebels without a Cause: What the Upsurge in Protest Movements Means for Global Politics," *Economist.* https://www.eiu.com/public/topical_report.aspx?campaign id=ProtestUpsurge.

3. The *Economist* Intelligence Unit, "Rebels without a Cause: What the Upsurge in Protest Movements Means for Global Politics," *Economist.* https://www.eiu.com/public/topical_report.aspx?campaignid =ProtestUpsurge.

4. Erica Chenoweth and Maria J. Stephan, *Why Civil Resistance Works: The Strategic Logic of Nonviolent Conflict* (New York: Columbia University Press, August 2011).

5. Manuel Castells, *Networks of Outrage and Hope: Social Movements in the Internet Age* (Cambridge: Polity, 2012).

6. Paul Mason, *Why It's Kicking Off Everywhere: The New Global Revolutions* (London: Verso, 2012), 3.

7. Fredric Jameson, "Future City," *New Left Review* 21 (2003): 76.

8. George A. Akerlof and Rachel E. Kranton, *Identity Economics: How Our Identities Shape Our Work, Wages and Well-Being* (Princeton: Princeton University Press, 2010).

9. Mason, *Why It's Kicking Off Everywhere*, 2.

10. Pierre-Joseph Proudhon, *General Idea of the Revolution in the Nineteenth Century* (New York: Cosimo, 2007).

11. Albert Hirschman, *Exit, Voice and Loyalty: Responses to Decline in Firms, Organizations, and States* (Cambridge: Harvard University Press, 1970).

12. Marcus Tullius Cicero, "Against Catiline," in *The Orations of Marcus Tullius Cicero*, trans. C. D. Yonge (London: Henry G. Bohn, 1856).

13. Daniel Smilov and Lea Vajsova, eds., *#The Protest: Analyses and Positions in the Bulgarian Press–Summer 2013* [*#Протестът. Анализи и позиции в българската преса–лято 2013*] (Sofia: Iztok-Zapad Publishing House, 2013).

14. Venelin Ganev, "The Legacies of 1989: Bulgaria's Year of Civic Anger," *Journal of Democracy*, 25 (1, 2014), 33–45.

15. Ho-fung Hung, *Protest with Chinese Characteristics: Demonstrations, Riots, and Petitions in the Mid-Qing Dynasty* (New York: Columbia University Press, 2011).

Chapter 2: The Democracy of Rejection

1. I owe this insight to the book of David Runciman, *The Confidence Trap: A History of Democracy in Crisis from World War I to the Present* (Princeton: Princeton University Press, 2013).

2. Runciman, *The Confidence Trap*, 23.

3. Moises Naim, *The End of Power: From Boardrooms to Battle-fields and Churches to States, Why Being in Charge Isn't What It Used to Be* (New York: Basic Books, 2013).

4. Pierre Rosanvallon, *Counter Democracy: Politics in an Age of Distrust* (Cambridge: Cambridge University Press, 2008), 176.

5. I am grateful to Professor Stephen Holmes for this insight.

6. Russell Brand, "On Revolution," *New Statesman*, October 24, 2013.

7. Alpha Research, "Public Opinion in Bulgaria, December 2013" ["Обществени нагласи в България. Декември 2013"], http://alpharesearch.bg/userfiles/file/1213_Public_Opinion_Alpha%20Research(1).pdf.

8. Alexei Slapovsky, *March on the Kremlin* [*Поход на Кремль. Поэма бунта*] (Moscow: ACT, 2010). Available at http://www.litres.ru/aleksey-slapovskiy/pohod-na-kreml.

9. Julia Ioffe, "The Loneliness of Vladimir Putin," *New Republic*, February 2, 2014. http://www.newrepublic.com/article/116421/vladimir-putins-russia-has-crushed-dissent-stillfalling-apart.

10. According to the pollsters at the Levada Center, 62 percent of the demonstrators on Sakharov Square had a university education. Andrei Soldatov and Irina Borogan, *Putin's Children: Flying the Nest*, oDR, 13 December 2011. http://www.opendemocracy.net/od-russia/andrei-soldatov-irina-borogan/putin%E2%80%99s-children-fly-nest.

11. Julia Ioffe, "The Potemkin Duma," *Foreign Policy*, October 22, 2009.

12. Sergei Kovalev, "Why Putin Wins," *The New York Review of Books*, November 22, 2007.

13. Soli Özel, "A Moment of Elation: The Gezi Protests/Resistance and the Fading of the AKP Project," in *The Making of a Protest Movement in Turkey #occupygezi*, ed. Umut Ozkirimli (Basingstoke: Palgrave, 2014, forthcoming).

14. Rosanvallon, *Counter-Democracy*, 65.

Chapter 3: Exit Politics

1. Albert O. Hirschman, *Propensity to Self-subversion* (Cambridge: Harvard University Press, 1995), 25.

2. Personal talk with protesters on the streets in Sofia.

3. Titus Livius Livy, *The History of Rome* (Books I–VIII), trans. D. Spillan, (New York: Digireads.com Publishing, 2009), 70.

4. Ivan Krastev, *In Mistrust We Trust: Can Democracy Survive When We Don't Trust Our Leaders?* (New York: TED Conferences, 2013), 47.

5. Alain Badiou, *The Rebirth of History: Times of Riots and Uprisings*, trans. Gregory Elliott (New York: Verso, 2012), 1.

Lightning Source UK Ltd.
Milton Keynes UK
UKOW03f1011200417

299528UK00001B/33/P